Lost Thunder

Lost Thunder

Poems

By David Galas

DARK RAVEN PRESS ■ SEATTLE

Published by Dark Raven Press
111 W. Comstock St.
Seattle, Washington 98119

Published in the United States of America

ISBN -13: 978-0-9841017-0-2

For the inheritors of time, the coming generation:

David and John, Arica and Anna, Michael,
Jenny, Emily and Laura, Joel, and David,
And for the next:

Caleb and Hayden

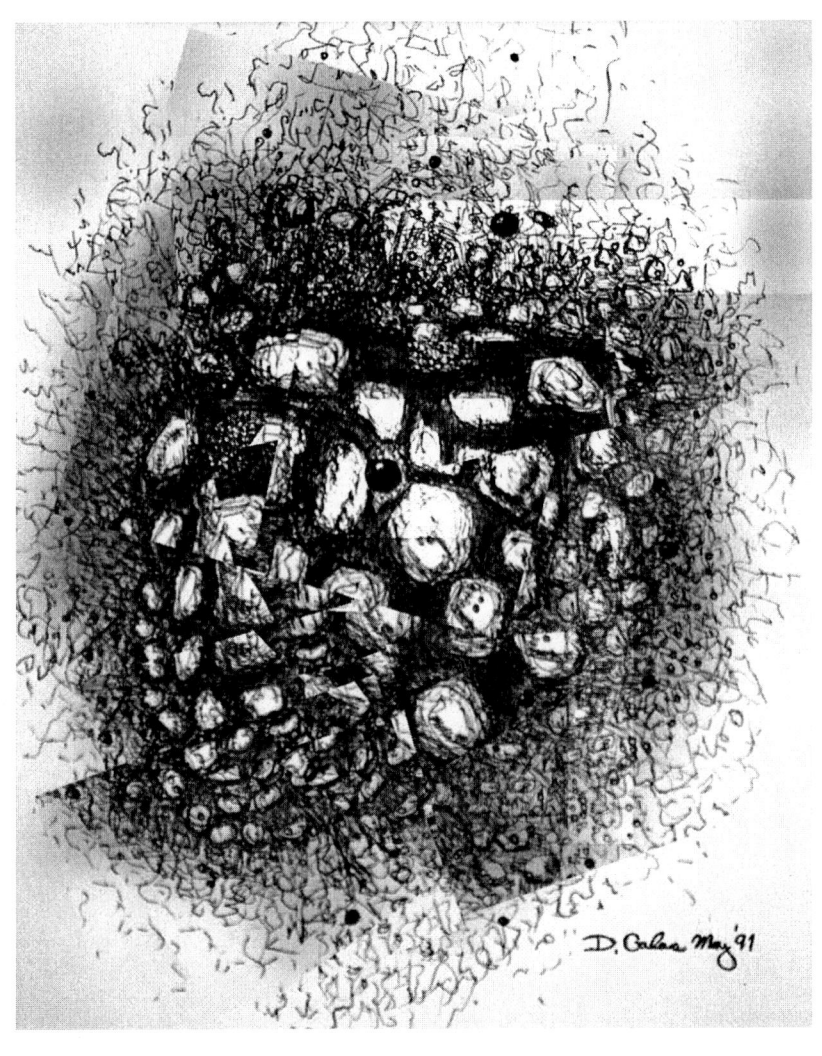

Contents

III.

…like lost thunder,
glaciers turning silver in late scattering of sun.
We were our later selves already,
wondering, all the way down.

-Tom Johnson

I.

When the wind stops and, over the heavens,
the clouds go, nevertheless
in their direction.

-Wallace Stevens

Science

Whatever it is it must have the strength
to stand against the weakness of our hearts,
to try our craft, and fire the silicon vitals
of our eccentric and small ambitions.

It speaks in breaths of beauty and in awkward truth,
to the sweep of galactic clouds, out of time's reach,
and in the pulse of intricate molecular purpose.
When we find it, it is immense, almost unseen,

and darkly fair. Roaring in splendid defiance,
it will roil the sea and sweep across the land.
It's fate will be to cruelly destroy, to build and love,
and to be lonely mid the hubbub of human minds.

***

Finding out

Finding out, when it works, is a joy.
less Eureka, than a deep
warmth that doesn't cool
in months of dull, hard days
and long nights, walking the halls
of eternity, bereft of love,
curiosity's fix.
More than darkness
set with galaxies.
What horizon is worth
the sense of relief that ends
in dim regret for lesser ends,
and not, as wished, in mixed
intent and euphoric stride,
across the room to have a look,
and finally to learn, again?

***

Painting

What is it in the semi-simple curve,
the charming middle twixt chaos and order,
that touches the eye and draws my mind into
a pleasant and forgetful land.

How you recoiled in disgust, thinking of
the grotesque symmetry of life's beginning and end,
the visible rise of an infant's mind each day,
and the risible loss of wit as time runs out,

and the unkind beauty of living out this pretty curve.
There is but one picture in the room, of a golden field,
a sky awash and a sharp cathedral thrust into
a cloud that is not too full, a land not too pleasant,

joined in canticles of colored strokes and ideas,
clustered in chaotic repose,
we yet despair of finding meaning in
the horizon's gentle curve,
and still we sing of beauty.

***

In the wake of the storm

As if a fearful power had passed,
the trees along the street recoiled,
drew back their shaking leaves and
stood perplexed in twisted branch.

The line of clouds regrouped to the west.
The wind played on with ill effect,
drew cold close to our bones, wrenching
cumulus circles, carrying fear into the fields.

Though no dust rose to sting our eyes,
I watched the silent, whirling
maple seeds descend deliberately,
heading east now on senseless gusts,
the trees' desperate bid to win the earth.

The ghost of hidden fear has now struck
its lethal bargain for which there is no reprise.
The scent of ozone on the wind is fresh,
but there is no recourse from this precious pact.

The seeds are gone to a thousand places,
the wind has died on the lips of evening's cry,
the fertile ground begins to heave
with gathering waves of the earth's dark passion.

***

Wildness

There's a wildness
in every refrain
from shouting out
in bitter anger,
in crowding moments
with singlular tastes,
inventing songs
from ordinary tears
and fragments of time,
in pacing mountains
and walking in fields
thick with silent
flowers not planted,
just touched and seen.

***

Rain Fell Today

Rain fell today into yesterday's space.
No sharp compulsion demanded
it be current – the present tensed anew.

Mist drifts like gravity was a guideline.
If it cease before the evening's onset
no one will care a whit forever dry.

I cannot see the glint of crinkling light,
as the soft air brightens a bit and then descends
into uncompromised darkness.

Waken soon, and know it's not too early or too late
for today's slender slice is all we can grasp.
The steel curtain of time is wet on both sides.

***

Lost Thunder

When I saw my teammate's letter
I heard again the soft snap of a twig,
felt the twitch of a far, bounding catch,
and listened again to murmurs of those rich seasons.

In an afternoon glass of wine
I saw the scarlet spring unwinding,
harsh echoes on the shouting fields,
following dreams of winning love,

winding up the threads of memory,
and the lost thunder of my former days.
The trees are less green now, and the grass browns to mud.
How will I find him on our shadowed pitch?

***

A black hole in a Paris park

When shadows move in staid array
above us as we stroll on the gravel and
the stone walls are spread thick with the light
of summer's solstice eve, we look back to see
the trees en bois subside and the leaves begin to die.
Have a drink, talk to me as life fades.
You have come back to Paris much too late.

Stare forlorn into the ancient glitter
of the city's welcome streets, the voice
of youth rising in your throat, and laugh
for what can never be again - the fierce warmth
of love's first thrust, the rattling pulse
of bright, new thoughts exploding in your head,
and the troubling promise of unending days.
sotto voce, et les enigme de tristesse.

As time begins to trickle into your waiting eyes,
in youth it collapsed in a moment's flash.
Don't forget, I saw you years ago walking here,
a pistachio cone in hand. You were a black hole,
exploding with boundless, silent light -
torn apart at the savage glow of time's horizon.
At your surface there was no time, no sleep,
no past or future, only the inside and out of you.

We discuss in murmurs the obvious paradox -
to where does timelessness disappear,
and when did it leave the scene?
Drink your pastis - it tastes almost the same.
Could it be the entropy of what you were?
You know, that's unavoidable, the cause
of your mass, your energy, your tender years.

We must now drink a salute to our
momentary transit through the point
where time stops and has no meaning,
as we have now arrived in the realm of time's
dominion, where it rules our weary dreams.

We morn the life of sleepless nights, and watch
the city beckon to others through its eternal tears.
You have come back to Paris much too late.

***

Undecideable Mountains

Breathless sweep of the logical plain
is broken by ranges of mountains.
Rugged and wild, their magnificent peaks
defy with lovely conundrums.
The slopes ascend in steep array
to fractal scarps and cliffs,
known only by alluring voice,
asking not when or how but if.

The hollow challenge "I am not proveable,"
echoes through lightless canyons,
then rolls off across the land.
It carries too on fickle winds,
and burns with a calculus
of bright and piercing thought,
to try the very limits of reason.

"If I am false then I am proved, and must be true,
since I cannot be both, I choose the truth.
But if I am true, I defy you completely."
Thereon lies impenetrable bedrock,
and the dark mountain rhyme defeats me.
Then "I am not proveable," finally, must be true.

Something is wrong in this, it seems
a theorem lost in the undecideable gleam
of the mountains – well before our time.
Can it be lost forever in darkness,
outside our world, outside of rhyme?
"I am not proveable," must always be true
by our own clever calculus, then by that
we first prove improveability.

Then are not Gödel's hulking peaks
utterly unreal? Or are they simply
engulfed in thick fictive mist?
Are the dark canyons and cliffs
just much more beautiful than we knew?

Speaking in recursive voice we hear
them echo with sounds that are almost human,
almost gone.

***

Mendeleev's Study

In such a small room tucked away at the base of the stairs
I could not see you, wedged among the clutter,
seeing in your mind, mid the whirl of madness,
alchemy's dreams, the magnificent table of matter,
arrayed in resplendent, regular rhythms.

How could you alone, old man, hear the sacred,
periodic notes, the partita of the galaxies,
while you sat, wondering on your ignorance,
desperate in that quiet, stifling study?
Was it just the saint of St. Petersburg
                              dreaming yet again?

I imagined you working in spacious comfort,
between warm, paneled walls on a wide, polished
table, a malchite vase with gold on the sideboard,
the codes of matter written on crisp pieces of paper,
spread in secret patterns on the glistening wood.

This only could befit the secrets that you plumbed
and gave to us who did not understand the dark,
clandestine purpose of the period patterns
pulsing, in the uncaring heart of the universe.

But the curious room was dusty and luminous,
with eccentric details enlisted to mark the utter
poverty of life – the smudged, ill-fitting windows,
a broken goose quill, a musty breeze when you stirred,
an ink-stained rug and a small perfect globe.

We could never imagine you there, alone and ill,
listening with ease to the music playing in that small room,
music you drew from the void with your heart,
chamber music never played to anyone before
who could hear like you, and now plays on
                              loudly forever.

***

25

Poseidon

A bright afternoon for eating fish and drinking
wine by the warm Aegean - eating even octopus,
we talked of loss and love and left drunk and laughing.

We lurched up the coast, baking in the sadness
of history's dumping ground, like searching rats,
ancient apotheosis of man.

Standing in the shadow of temples, thirsting on
the dusty hill, I came to see what was left
of my belief in Poseidon at Sunion's point.

The coins of sunlight glittered on the sea,
priceless lucre of our present that cannot
pay the debt of yesterday's foolish tricks.

The bus came at sunset, releasing crowds
to whoop at the setting sun, to stare at the
dirty marble, and be moved as I could not be.

On that sequined sea the king's son came back,
to incompetence and death, as we do, I thought,
but what can I do now ? It happened so long ago.

Down the hill there are milk white fragments
of time lying under bushes, patiently dying.
The sea's revenge is awful, but always amusing.

***

The Filling of the Moon

Once as a child I watched the moon fill from half to
full.
In a flash, it gave me to fully understand,
how it's done, or so I thought.
If I had doubted, now it was clear that god must
be the one who shaped the light and threw the
switch,
and it really must be true, for I had seen it,
or so I thought I had. Once.

*** *

Autumn sortie

The tree-sieved wind tumbles down the island's flank
across the slate cold water to where all month
the ducks and grebes rode out the anger of the storms.
Their fleet in battle formation arrays its many minions.

Riding low they breast the blow, and heave to hold their ranks.
To the left a convoy of canvas backs wheels to starbord,
and heads into the break, a mobile squadron closing up.
With their chins to chests they look like bits of wood.

Turning into the wind they gather their force and launch
across the wave tops, fully armed, rising together,
and close up now dropping low, turn along the swell
and disappear, flying fast on their deadly mission.

***

When Kite was king

I can taste the raw thickness
of the wind and see myself
walking blown beside you.

I am dangled by my kite
into this dangerous world below,
and drug along the meadow's face.

I am the bait that might entice
those gorgeous monsters
of the earth to surge from their lairs

and impale themselves in blind
and bloody strikes at the demons
of heaven that assail their hours.

My kingfisher, royal trapezoid
of tissue paper and sticks, loves them all
in his dances, tugging at my string,
tantalizing fate for his sweet purpose.

The capricious wind holding us
up from above could stop and plunge
us unprepared into the deadly richness
of the wanton chaos reigning here below.

***

Annelids and Crustaceans

On the end of the day's run,
at the tide's utter ebb,
he stood at the open door, facing west,
and watched the gulls in silence
sweep the sun-sprayed mud, avid,
searching for incautious worms and crabs.

The dance of evening's illusion went on
as he stepped through the door, and
coming to the beach, walked
in his imagination
on polygons of light,
searching for survivors.

***

Heron Island lagoon

Daybreak on Heron Island

Umber wings tear the grey cloud wall,
cumulus spawned by the warm dark sea,
feathered scythes slash the sky, while
the south wind rises and night comes apart,
our sea is cyan streaked and dirty with white.

As far as I can see the coral flats recede
before the tide – green, white and living brown,
luminous air leaks into the wounds of the sky
and makes them bleed to cinnabar and rose.
Blood draws the gaunt shadow birds by thousands
above the lagoon from the beach brush and pisonia.

And yet ... the soul of Heron is coral,
variegated, bulbous, antlered, blue, pink, bristling,
pointed, blunt and broken, rubble and sand,

alive and dead with fulminations
of living stone – miles of ornamented reef molded
to the fine compulsive eye of the demented sculptor.

The stars, now gone, were strange to me,
transported to the planet Heron,
 in the Capricorn system, light years from home.
I walked on their skeletons, mourning
for the encircling, life-draped rocks that
had begun to think of the day to come.

***

An idea

The enchantments of reason bridge
chasms of myth, and wild rivers
of white raging sentiment.
Across time and country a shining
idea loves you hard with a passion
that sees the fine shadow's edge
in each glimmer of thought,
and smooth contour's feel –
but, tell me, can it still be alive?

I don't see your sad, slumped shoulder,
still at evening, or the wan frown
of our pale and gentle inclination.
Where were you when night shaded
that fine laughing look,
from their cynical stares?

The notion spans even my time,
and in each of our discerning,
passing years, recapitulates and lasts.
The light of guarded lamps is seldom seen.

***

Never tree dreams

I am a forester.
The green earth here has wet shadows,
the light is gold and blue.
Moss thickens umber and ferns curl
tight beneath my boots,
the heavy musk of wood.

I walk in deep shade where
the red soil turns mud of naked earth
into the blood of ancient trees,
the stumps smell soft as death's breath.

Green bleeds, oozing slow,
thunder and long flailing limbs,
the crack of saplings' backs and tear
of branches whips the forest floor,
kiss the sounds of hills and wind's refrain.
Trees becoming timber logs.

I am not a forester, forever

35

find me beneath the dying mass
of fallen trees, senseless to touch,
after two hundred years, at last the earth's embrace.

Daylight flows over armored flanks.
Tree voices moan from my throat,
crying for times now so distant.   Wind and rain
wail the wood's death song. Fill my veins with pungent sap,
and follow the calls of sun-loving birds,
that fly now like dreams we'll never see.

***

Wood Ducks

A pair of wood ducks arrived today
on the warm breath of vernal change.
Preening in the sun, his bright white stripe,
his glistening feathered helmet,
made it seem rude to watch
him wear himself so for the world
and his dull duck wife,
touched by the hand of heaven.

A heavy hand, green and strong,
marks him for the splendor
of an unknown fortune,
until his rising power
and the peak of summer
declines in mystic measure
into the chill arctic air
and the grey autumnal void.

He followed her awkwardly
across the bright new grass as if he
wondered the color of her eyes,
The cold, blue water wrinkles in the
glint of color from his wing.
I see him rise now, churning fast
to the west, where the sun goes.

I can track his flight across the bay

where other restless beasts begin to stir.
  Their dark company becomes a chorus
To the rising of this season's song.
  For now he flies alone and straight,
  Vividly on still resplendent wing.

***

Snow Not Sticking

The flakes of tomorrow's whiteness
chased in spiral course descend.
Each tiny crystal struck the ground and
sucked the warmth in latent heat
from the darkening soil.

In morsel by tiny morsel
the warmth of the earth is eaten by
countless fragments of heaven
dying on its ragged face.

It's not a pretty sight, more like
an awful accident of weather, I'd say,
or a swarm of those aggressive bees,
turning in mutant fury to kill
the bystanders meaning them no harm,

Brownish gore and wet slush everywhere
until it begins to stick – and then
it could take your breath without killing,
like the beauty of tomorrow seen from

A distant time, when the earth is dead white,
and today the crystalline mites fall dormant,
covering our many sins in ice,
waiting for just the right moment.

***

Genomes' Faces

Rock strata tell the past if you ask them.
Speak the old words, dead echos ago,
that mark the levels of the sea and past climatic fates.
It was all different then, nothing like the urgent
call of today's twice ghostly face.

But the genome is a magical thing, Janus-faced,
enigma's thread, long yesterday's tale speaks
then too the bloody promise of future might or may.
There is no thing that tells both fables, faces
past and future, imprints of then and away,
yet the story winds on back and forth, unending.

The soul of man lies in the whence from which
He comes, and the where to which he goes,
Alone and together with all the muttering others.
The wretched grief, the soaring pain,
the blanket of time, the bloody refrain,
it's written in careless strokes, a line
that wounds the heart in two ways.

***

My vacation

If you could be here to see
the distant, humped shadows
come riding in close at noon,
blue silhouette mountains,

the stuff of dreams in youth,
source of madness in age,
and always being beautiful,
you would know what happened.

Why did I come here again?
For the heat, or expectation,
squinting in the morning, swimming
and sweat, waiting for the evening wind?

And through it all the season ripens,
dark orchards of fruit swell slowly
and sweet, the sea riffles with breeze,
and then with a thunder clap, it happens.

Though the world was shattered
the daylight hours were still clear,
like the air of far, sun-raked
hills after a violent rain.

Intimations of elegiac whispers
lingered in my mind like wishes,
but the bright shards of sky lay
scattered like stones around my feet.

Night was worse, but more lovely,
I could see the special things
that matter in solemn darkness,
like the staring stars, descending
in swarms to see what happened.

Each day it takes my breath away,
and I wish you were here, to see
what I cannot. Though it has happened,

41

the days and nights go ever smoothly on,

as if I were just the same, as if I didn't know
that the world is too perfect to be etched
by time, or marked by life's wandering track.
When I return next season to feel the sun
we'll both know what happened then.

***

The magic room

My uncle told me once of a magic room,
a remarkable place he saw once when
he was young, a cloistered room of secrets,
immuring time as well as space.
Two times he was shown the room.

It seemed like once - it was always familar.
He touched the walls and felt the heat of time.
He stalked in a trance, turning towards the center,
the remnant core of what remains at the heart of meaning,
gazed on the metallic mesh that embraced the
precious shards of lost treasures at the center.

What was it that hushed the room,
left it so hungry for living thought?
By cryptic measure he marked his way,
carefully, slowly, as traces of his passing
faded to receding hours at the edge of the room.

They merged with the magic meter of the final,
entropy of uncle's thoughts. He came away,
but to this day he has never been the same, nor
do I expect he'll ever stop searching to align
the door he saw in secret so long ago,
listening for the utter silence of his captive time,
and looking for yesterday's tomorrow.

***

Monkey reaching for the moon in the water

Would he be less for wanting
to be human, like the artist?
He hangs suspended in silken
strokes of imagination's brush,
clever marks of long descent
from a branch above the still
water's precious glass.

Ekaku left him at the mercy
of our mind's voracious eye
for more than a thousand years.
He is a magical creature that
lives in time and does not die.

The fingers of his hand extend.
His discontent with the surface
reaches deep, cold beyond
for the image of the moon's pale face.

The new moon dawns tonight
for the ten thousanth time,
and yet he has not touched it.
I stare in silence from across the room.
The smooth, golden scroll reaches
from the ceiling to the floor.

***

Archadean episodes

"But it's just like Septimus to spout that nonsense,
all about the perfect spheres and clockwork curves
that no longer delight us in their symmetrical beauty,"
she said, genuinely distressed by his failing to see.
She whirled about laughing, traced a complex curve,
glanced back with tilted head, and sunk on bended knee.

In his eyes, crystal epicycles ground to a stop and dissolved,
confronted by her graceful neck and the chaos of her silken gown.
Long hair set with a golden clasp, downward glance of disavowed
understanding, wide eyes of crystalline, dark innocence,
waiting, like the thawing earth of springtime's breath, for him,
who does not understand at all what she cannot help but sense.

The mathematic of nature was glimpsed only in shadow
by those ancients, with their glittering eyes. Their cones
and sections that I must revere, she thought, are bland and smooth
where the trees are shagged with form and warm as fractal fur.
Seeing like Fermat did, she could only make a joke, for the margins
of her life could not contain the proofs she could not secure.

The geometric form of reason's shape is not matched against
imagination's random turns, it turns within and repeats the words
until erratic edge collides with itself and regularity relents.
Imagination's erratic shape wanders by simple direction,
but simplicty lies at the heart of romantic self-delusion.
Her voice echos still through the random trees, calling for him.

On a crisp autumn day, wandering on a wooded path,
I have seen the falling leaves - they are all the same, almost.
Have you wondered too at the shapes of weeds, and the chaos
of frightened expectations, worried by the muddied earth,
rich in unexpected form, waiting and longing for the light
to shatter the deathly grasp of night's unreasoning hold?

He and I know that it never can, but there is nothing for it.
The leaves will fall and grow again next year - it is quite simple.
A candle dimly lights a page of our most desperate poetry,
he tries to read, but he hears her call from the depths of his dreams
and his enlightened mind must listen to the music of her voice,
the notes follow each other, wondering why
                                    it seems so simple now.

(an homage to Tom Stoppard)

***

Boating on a slow river

Reeds whisper to water's flow,
and scuds of driven clouds, speaking
unseen beauty that lies deep in the
ordinary face of this damp and forgotten
land, where life pulses ever on, regardless,
breeding throngs of tiny restless things.

This is a song that can't well be sung
but by you who live with creatures of the damp.
We can sing it, false sometimes, feigning truth
in our fear of being found out,
found to be dry and clean and naive at heart.
Our potted flowers whisper lies to the wind
who will not believe and call them slaves.

If I talk of the river, insist I tell it all,
not only of the lovely day boating,
but the embarassing story of
the grounded boat, pried free from the mud.
now floating free, smeared with the foul, black
muck of a thousand silent years –
stinking in its fame, teeming with intricate
life in filth and hope – now it becomes common.

At evening, when cold shadows invade the land,
and light is lost among the reeds, darkening
relentless, gentle flow will mark our time,
and stir the reeds into whispers of our passing.
All that matters now is that it's truly said.
I can hear the sounds of the river sometimes,
when day is caught and spread upon the bank.
We smile to see it so – it looks small and
profligate, irresistible, sad
                   and forever gone.

***

II.

Beautiful my desire, and the place of my desire.

- Theodore Roethke

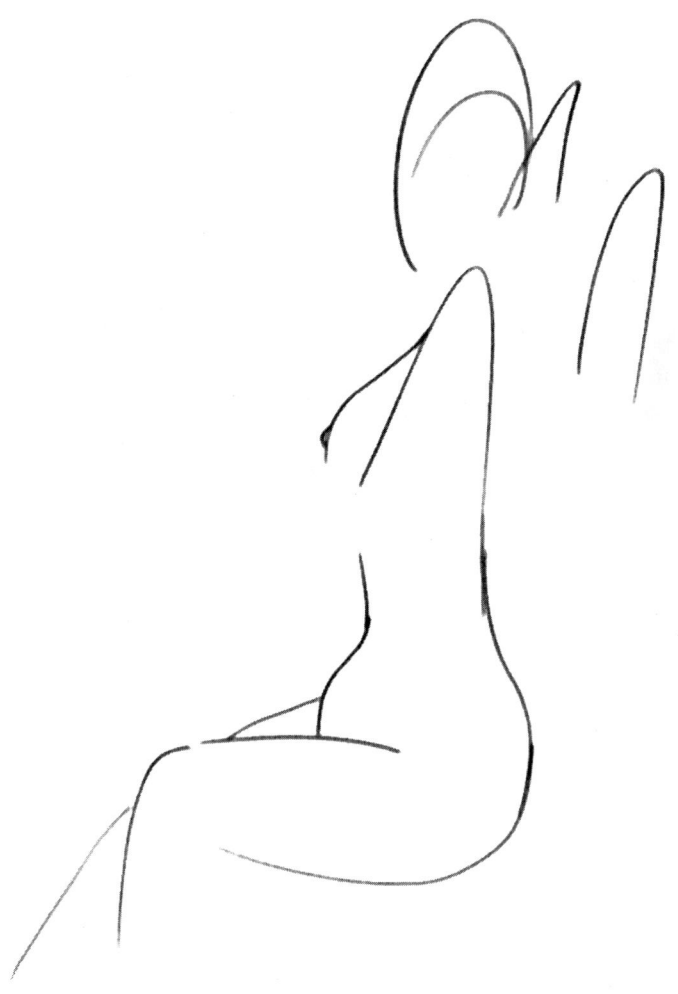

The Mold of Spring

In diluted light this morning's damp,
the mold of spring was born.
It smells a promising death
I had mercifully forgotten.
The brown hillside is soon consumed.

Complex chemical promise,
all the souring richness,
seeps from the warming ground.
Iconic clouds mark the morning's
intent, and rush off into vapor.

Liturgy of years past arise,
the stubbled field heaving clods,
dank, aged, dark and fragrant.
In wonder I sense your voice afresh,
on the scent of new ferment.

The fumes draw out all our tired dreams,
since I am only the sum of all the good
that I will ever cause to be,
all the evil halted, dark illumined,
less the sum of all the pain.

If you had walked here
long ago, and called to me,
I could recall the musty sweetness now
smelling the hint of green at
the tips of twisted branches.
Until today I was safely cold
in the thrall of crowded stars.

***

Lake Quintet

I.

The wind wrinkles the
face of autumn's water,
and blows dead leaves,
into winter. Change
is what is left behind.

II.

You have been gone so long
I cannot remember the sound
of your voice, your being near.
I cannot take my eyes from
the single tree across the lake.

III.

In my dreams the hours pass
like frost in the morning.
Neither can I see your face
in the deep black water.
A bird passes far out on the lake.

IV.

An eagle stopped here today
with his fish. He ate slowly
and drank in the weak sun.
Crows flew at him, screaming.
When he had eaten he left.

V.

Evening shrouds my house
with migrant mists.
In the garden they wet
the icy stones. Inside,
thinking of tomorrow,
I light a lamp and wait for
my cloak of dreams.

Know love?

You've loved, no?
You know what it means?

You know French?
But what about Sartre?

The wood's smoothest
touch comes just
before the splinter's gash.

The lustrous gaze
of winter's glow,

A touch of blood,
the lovely cold,

I think you know
but will not tell me.

***

Hawkins Hill

Soon I'll stand on Hawkins' hill
and sieve your heart, your feet, your bones
through my fingers, and think of you,
but not as you are now.

I'll see you riding hard,
Taut in the cold wind,
heart-pumped blood in your flesh,
your face turned to laugh,
to shout to me who wondered if I could
feel like that and hold you tight
with these dusty fingers.

Soon I'll wait for the wind to rise
and throw your ashes upward
as hard as I can, and watch
the dust drift down on the woods
to the weeping river.
You'll never be more real to me
nor farther away than now.

Listen to the murmurs of time
in your thudding pulse
and see the glint of soon on your golden
hair.
Then I'll stand still on Hawkins' hill
and sob, remembering now and your caress,
hanging on as you disperse and how we
made love
this afternoon on Hawkins hill.

***

Your Death and Mine

Between your death and mine
will fall some long, rare days of sun,
cold rain, mornings, afternoons,
hard winds that scrape the face,
steel glint of the lake in March, perhaps,
sweet grass smells from warming mud,
deep aches of a missing friend,
and ever light embracing the dark
green earth in which lies yours or mine.

***

To an old woman

When I think of her blue-white cotton dress
flowing round my face like the sky in a summer wind,
I hear her voice singing for me, her warm breast,
sour smell and a gush of irrational love,
her bony hand and murmur that has no rhyme.

She spoke of times and things I longed to see, and sank
the arc of winter's sky in the grasp of her arms.
She was a border camp to the refugee heart, heart's blood to
those who, with blood on their faces, watched life flee in fear.
No less strong, she breathed in anguish and exhaled freedom's air.

And now awash in desperate strife and calls for justice,
in a cold rain from the sea, we pull our coats tighter,
and with an eye to the rear call to her for tyranny's end.
Her silent answer draws in all the air, all the sea
       and shattered light
into a fierce and godless sound – she sings her long dream
whose echo cannot be heard among the living.

***

Cocktail Hour

March with me through the day's complexities,
sing along as we mouth the words we thought we knew.

At the end, the cocktail hour, in a well-lit room,
the piano picks out just the notes that Satie chose.

Say those things to her, again, but musical sounds
of indistinct meaning, a subterfuge of logical force.

Sound the triumphant fare, echo the history of the day.
The power of the message and its meaning is not lost

among the trees of mute witness, shadow embrace,
The sparkling jewels, the burbling murmur of water,

the concealing gesture, and the meaningless glance.
The tangle of beaten paths confuses the trail of intent,

small flowers, unseen in dark corners of the forest floor,
The leaves so small, the pollen green, the surrogate lips.

I want to pick them now and in the cartography of longing
discover a kiss of stone that lay untouched for years.

***

Life on the Edge

Life on the edge is as it's lived
by most – it's short, maybe sweet,
a flashing wave, a shifting smile,
a fever of longing for
everything and another while.

Can this intricate path
wind between the vacuum
and the staring blank eye of the sun,
whose light is life and warmth?
At the edge, and beyond, it still moves us,

A course like the edge
of a sharp cone of light.
How precise can we be today?
How fine the edge that I drew,
the morning I first saw you smile.

***

Love is like a lot of things

You are too much like time,
too patient, and just too dark,
like my grandfather's friend.
Too much like too many
others I have tried
to really know, to taste,
to spend those small hours
in painful remembering
the silence of her skin,
the sharp smell of darkness
in the consuming night.

Love is like a lot of things,
but flawlessly hard,
like steel, and too dark too.
It devours me like
a new idea of beauty.
The force of her breath,
too strong to resist,
seeped into my blood
much too warm and gentle,
so slow, so soft like skin,
it began like music.

The breath of time is just
like that, like love, and
before it nothing stands,
nothing waits in silence.
It is too much to expect,
     like a lot of things.

***

The Spider of Your Love

The venom be quashed by the dance,
a whirling fling of drifting silk and
gravel heels strike the stone floor.
I'm far past tired and near,
drained of vision's sweet drink,
still it tastes of death, my dear.

No cure from tarantella,
lingering on, ever darker
beneath the skin, crawling
in the veins of my arms, my days
are spun in sunlight and the sea,
and nights we live in the colors
af hours, scarlet, blue and black.

The sounds of seconds marching
to my fingers, deep in the bite.
it's not so much the pain or frenzy,
but delight in not knowing how
it will end – in fire or freezing,
a soft muffled laugh or
in my gentle strangulation.

The astonishing mutter in my ear,
the counter rhythm of your blood
is all I want to hear, but now I can't.
My pulse flutters, my placid heart
listens and puzzles the spreading
sheen of my blood on the stone.

Explain to the crowd the clear
compulsion of dancing forms,
that live and die without knowing how

we keep our fires banked, our flame
shielded from the wind, in case of
danger, in case of blood, in case
we come on love and dance on
in the spinning pall of darkness.

***

Weekend's End

Late Sunday afternoon, near the end of summer
comes the longing for days just past, regret
for what, in the fullness of time, I didn't do.
Sometimes summer ends like this.

Low sun strikes, and shattered light from the lake
makes us pull the curtains and think of brighter hours,
when the full force of prolix summer ruled.

The past's shadow more imagined future,
you never dodge its insistent claim, wishing
for more days with an ache like being away.

Just the sleepy calm at weekend's end,
draws glimpses of light remembrance,
like awkward family films that make me look away.

She cleaned the house deep in her own darkness
while I read the papers and watched for her wit,
like a tickling feather or embracing smile.

All summer I wondered why the warmth of her heart
glowed so weakly now, holding back the evening's blood,
but the wall was breached and shadow poured in.

This afternoon for a moment I thought I knew why.
The wind pushed aside the curtain for the last of the sun,
she looked far beyond the lake to the fading hills,
                                   shielding her eyes.

***

Just a While Longer

It's getting late and the afternoon is gone.
The wolves of memory gather to hunt.
The light so intense it hides your face,
Your eyes, and all your secret wishes.

A silver coat of mail lies on the water's breast,
Protecting the world from arrows of thought.
The world's water blunts those vicious darts,
but the pack is restless, closing in.
Stay with me here,
        stay now a while longer.

Knowing how I miss you so, but
how I hate the world you see,
I shield my eyes and you're gone, devoured
by the wolves, your face, your eyes,
        my memories of your flesh.

The trees are as black as the night forest's breath.
I see nothing afoot, but hear them padding by.
They are not sated and must kill again.
It's getting late, the sky is fading, please,
you must stay here
        just a while longer.

***

Fly

Somehow, a fly had got in.
It coursed the room and bumped
the window's haze, sounding
like a nasty question,
excited by the sun.

And when you rose, alone at last,
to leave, I marked the place
to start tomorrow.
It's hard to keep this up,
love's languid pace

belies the weakness
of the heart. You stoop
to find an elusive shoe,
look quickly back
at the buzzing sound.

It's not so much the time
but that we're deadly tired.
I lie askew and watch
the door. The fly is well gone
before darkness comes.

***

The lake at night

On the dock I sit for hours in the moonlight.
Dreaming, I wait for the moment that never comes.
Watch the long waves of glass pass beneath me.
There seems nothing beneath dark water,
deep nothing, and places I can never go.
In the morning they will be gone forever.

Geese by the willows speak softly to each other,
lamenting song sighs that they too must
soon be gone, must leave this place like you.
In the warmth of this dim night nothing happens,
I think of you slipping, without a ripple,
into the chill vacuum beneath black lake waters.

I feel the lake weed waving lightless down below,
to me, to you, I miss you so.

***

Face

Come with me,
At last embraced,
A warm entwined, but
longing face, far away.
Sweet muddling on,
Thinking of yesterday.

Remarkable glance,
an amazing face,
eyes so tightly fixed.
I think I begin
to see you now,
and pretty nice.
Almost too beautiful
          to see.

***

Afflictions of a fictle heart

Jewelled tokens of my affection
for myself lie scattered on the rug,
in witness to long troubled hours
of dying I have done in your name.

They sparkle brightly, speaking books
of approximations to love, allegories
singing adoration, life's golden hook,
and the web of dacron dreams, dedicated

to what none but a fictle heart knows well.
It fulminates secretly, and is molded
in hallowed hours of summer's endless light,
against the bitter dying of the night.

I call to you for what must be one last time,
like perplexing sounds of complex rhymes,
for your precious life and soon forgotten joy.
My only solace is in that far windy place
where, until now, I thought no one ever goes.

***

Breasts

My eyes reach out to touch
that fulsome, downy shape
they cannot comprehend -
your breasts in longing
dreams, warm textures,
knives of silken promise rise,
when, pressed against my brain,
they yield and cover
all with metaphors of life.

Your skin will flush and sweat in throes of love
as tiny seeds of cancer's iron will
within weave their merciless plot
of betrayal to conquer in time
all that our passion has ever claimed,
the turn of your head, a caress,
your life, my eyes, my mind.

***

Soul bones

She's not happy today and
the bones of her soul protrude.
They rise to the surface of her
skin where every touch
evokes exquisite
pain.

Far away the strains
of sour music make her grind
her teeth, exceeding all
the fine power of patience,
with a lifetime's store
used and spent.

And nothing anywhere seems to help.
The smoking bits of her dreams
lie nearby, I think she has left
the gentle fold of my arms
forever, and the bones of my soul
begin to break
    to bits.

***

On Twenty Years Without my Friend

His jowled face I'll never greet, support his halting step,
neither will we regret growing old over our whiskey,
nor flash a grandson's photo in the evening sun.
If we met he'd leap two steps at once and excuse my
tired embrace, he'd pronounce his harsh critique of
poets whose very names I have forgotten.
Come, memory, let me seek him there in the shadows.

(after Donald Justice)

***

A child's England

I see her still in mind's recess
in a dark, chill mist she
lives on unreformed.
Green quilted, cruel land,
kingdom of latent dreams,
stitched with hedgerows,
sunless rivers wandering slow,
oozing beneath belted skies.

Hedgerows hide the eggs of birds
who fly from our forced affection.
I smell it now, the dark nest musk
that seduces us, craving eggs and
the scent of blood and procreation,
spawning our lust for speckled
shells on soft, thymic meadows
and in the hard thorny bush,
where we hid from grownup eyes.

I see them still, flashing
their yellow chaffinch wings
that mock dank meadows,
to fly free, to nest
and die under love's
solemn good intent, cold
gold emblem of young ardor's
reach. Now I know they
are no more – did we kill them?

The wet fog swelled come morning,
like cold bedclothes, its foul
damp dressed us
so completely that
streetlamps, tall buses,
brick houses and grey, stone schools
were sucked into another world.
As I walked in grim and guilty dreams
Each day wandering the path
To school, a wreath of

Filthy mist around my face.

The swelling music now stops
My throat with rare sorrow
at the soft, icy rain of what
passed for love and what
fully enfolded my heart
in the winter of our
life's beginning.
Lessons learned in wisdom,
and at the lash of a bamboo cane
can never be forgotten.

The pain of cold awoke me.
I dressed in coughing anger
at a bloody throat
in the dark morning's
most solemn moments,
clothed in strange attire.
At first I could not understand
the lilt of their tongues,
stiff linen napkins and silver rings
without a taste of eggs and butter.
I knew well then the stark,
icy hand of God and England,
or who they said was god,
deep burning sorrow, shame
hope, love and glory smiles.

I fought and bled from the nose
and knee in puzzled anguish,
and inglorious delight each day,
these young primeval years.
But it all came clear when we
finally burned Guy Fawkes.
Our bonfire of muddled
purpose raged defiant,
flared in red-yellow flame
and died dancing in the frigid
 night, resounding to our joy,
blazing hot on the brow
of later grassy hills,

to the shouts of dangerous friends.

The sun of spring can heal
the knees and draw
us to the bluebell woods
to hide in the sudden warmth
of May, to learn the flowers,
to lick your neck, to find new birds.
We sought to banish the fog
 and seek bright solace
that later would find us
lying in damp bracken beds,
clutching at English wool-sheathed
hearts to fight the steely cold,
      and forget the birds.

***

Parents

You worshiped the small, evil god
that I was - fat, grotesque, insistently
pink and filled with the promise
of your destiny, poor things.
The milk wet breast of mom
gave me that one thing I needed.

When the colorless face I loved began
to shift, the rapturous pact mid
past and future, like heady perfume,
enveloped us all in confusion.
The roaring freight of morning struck
the night and shattered all that I remember.

Brilliant fragments now drift through our days
like jewels from distant time. I think of you
often, the way you tried to tell me of your
love, your pain, and say those things, clear
your throat and change the way you spoke,
and now you can no longer change.

***

Photo of a girl

She looks to future days now past,
bright face, summer dress bold in the grey face
of war's grim pallor, just before I met her.
She smiles in fear for hers and my life:
1943 was a good year.

If she saw me then, my childish sorrows,
melodies played on dark strings in times,
dead real to her, now mythic to me, our breath
Not yet mingled, the smoldering of Europe.
Her husband so soon to leave her then.

He was to fly the high flak fields of the Ruhr,
where her life would soon be suspended
in the breathless puffs of black – white contrails,
stark straight in abstractions of death's chance,
of the tearing end of life's sweet sampling.

What did her clear eyes know of that?
The beauty I remember well, soft eyes for me
And all her children, dressed like fragile creatures

of awkward tales from times yet to come.

I can feel those hands, those hands touch my face.
 In English spring gardens she stuck a carnation,
 just plucked, in my lapel before church.
Warm new days, like flowers from the earth,
made her sing, murmuring those tunes, grasping
the day with the hold of one who, having dodged
war's cruel and random blows, forgets all else.

I hear her young voice humming badly, burned into me,
Walking the later rooms of her life's unraveling.
The photo shows only the impatient, enfolding arms
that would, intently evading the vagaries of life's
violent charms, carefully hold her grandchildren.

I think she imagined in dreams what she could not
understand, that she and I, surviving being born, could
never live in blacks and grays again. Colored daubs
paint in precious tears our measures of meaning.
I see the bright color of a summer dress, a turning laugh.

The leaves that shook that day have disappeared.
They stood in her gardens, then swept by the wind,
they shivered briefly for her innocence, and were gone.
Wandering in still remembered scenes, I hear again
And again the warm, hard words that left her lips.

She paints a magical image of both our youths,
as near the end she spoke of things from the time
when she was gone. Another myth, like the golden
melodies she wove through our lives, undaunted
she sternly folded her arms, and humming softly,
fled from time on the wings of her innocence.

(*written on 31 July 1992, the day of my mother's death*)

***

76

Funerary pomp

"... And in the lives of men, irreversible.
And it seems a relief. To win? To lose?
What for if the world will forget us anyway?"
- Czeslaw Milosz

In that same mocking church
I walked forward across
the colored tile, in the light
of dedicated squares
of garish glass. I had stood
and knelt here long before
in aching ennui and the pride
of a child's metamorphosis -
fixed on future days afar,
inhaling the incense.

I walked again just now,
in bracing grief, old and tired,
to the lectern of ludicrous
pronouncements, luscious lies,
to speak the truth of my father,
as last year of my mother -
to squeeze the tasteless words
forcibly from my mouth.

I can speak now, having
kissed their cold foreheads.
The chill still on my lips, I can
speak of what he was and why,
and how we have come to this time
and place, walking solemnly through,
but I can't be sure I'm right.

I reach to touch his hand
a last time, and see his stoic face
with a hint of a smile from his
 sunken cheeks - his last joke?
Leaning in, I see his makeup.
Suddenly the coffin and church seem strange,
familiar, and impossible to grasp.

Even the painted statues are moved.

Talk, hushed, to the efficient priest,
and thank him unaccountably for what?
Saying nought rather than foolish things?
For what, I think, wanting to laugh
out loud and sob with my sons and sisters.
Why are we here but to laugh and sob?

The colors here are much brighter
than I remembered, and the place
much smaller still. The vaults are pinched
and less beautiful than then,
than how I wanted them to be,
or will ever be again.

So did you hear him, hear the
singing or talking in the other room?
Was it just the echo of lingering recall?
Don't kid me now. You know that now
the awkward young men, are marching,
then they'll fire their weapons
at the harsh command, and stand
ill-at-ease, shifting from foot to foot.
They were not born when I was here last.

Stand still as the bugle notes fade
away to before, fondly and a bit too fast
for us to grasp their passing.
Did you hear him, did you remember it all?
The wind is now colder than my lips,
as memory dissolves. It is just too late.
The priest who didn't know him departs.

Could it be that it will ever come again?
Can we remember his darkling past?
It looks like rain today, and we have to go,
to leave him here, the light is fading fast.
Auden says it takes eighteen months
to ripen a skeleton, to be rid
of the burden of mortal flesh.

He may be right, but try to think
of her last year at just this place,
the lady of the gate, as he said, beneath
that stone. Will father know, will he
be surprised to see her so?

Memory sublimates without regret, like a whiff
of incense, or a touch, another voice
from another room, barely heard, or
no better than he would guess after all.
So please just don't kid me anymore.
His life is done, be honest, don't forget
it's too late now and dinner's waiting

***

Godfather

When I asked my father about him he was slow
to find the words – "he was a good Italian boy."
His voice was soft when he spoke of Ralph,
his roommate at West Point, mostly,
I gathered, because they were short together.
Staring from a photo now they seem almost sad,
determined, scared, at attention in front of tent,
in their funny hats, their chests swelled, with pride
most likely, with rifles and cavalry puttees.
Were they wondering when they could get to New York?

Living for three hard years had made deep creases
on dad's soul that never seemed to fade. But I don't know
so much about Ralph, he's told me so little.
He died just a few years later the records show.
One cold winter in France he stepped on a German mine.
I don't know what his heart was like, or would have been.
I think of him only as an old man, my father's friend,
but he was never older than my son.

Think of him as Lieutenant Ralph Renzouli, dark and young,
eager soldier, scared, confused, but my father's fast friend.
I can think of him smiling at my mother. I can think of him
lying in the Ardennes snow screaming for the corpsman.
"Where the hell are you? My leg is gone, I'm aging fast."
I think of him thinking of me, what would I be like,
this infant godson of his? His leg spurting blood.
Christmas day of the year I was born father flew from England
To stop the Germans in the forest before they got to Ralph,

But he was too late, and he couldn't find him anyway.
I think of Ralph with graying hair, drinking Campari, talking to me
about the bad winter of '44 when the Germans almost got him,
about the mine, or was it a bullet, that wounded him,
his ticket home, and how he got to see me then.

The young are godfathers to the old, it seems.
What are you, aged decades in a single year, no memories?
I should give him some good advice, He deserves it,
and after all I lived so much longer than Ralph.

***

III.

A little knowledge, a pebble from the shingle,
A drop from the oceans: who would have dreamed
this
 infinitely little too much?

- *Robinson Jeffers*

A Poet's Fate

The world does not need you - know it the hard way,
by gathering shards of the living science of the earth,
beneath the fluent light of sunsets and dawns, untouched
by deceptive stones and tiny fragments of fictive affect,
my life, yours and astringent wine, late in dark enclose.
It all seems to fit somehow, an image of pure illumination,
unchanged by your departure, yet knowing that changes all.

Feel the sporadic breeze and hear the sound of being just the same.
Were the weather to amend the world the day after your death,
I would not find it strange, and yet you would never know. Words that
quartzine facets transformed beyond hearing:
the geology of living stores the subtle marks of the human voice in rock.
Both light and sounds, and the echos of this sedimentary language
we summon from the hot magma of our dreams – and I hear you well.

The sunlight of tomorrow doesn't know you, nor will it soften pain.
The world does not need you, but aches somewhere deep inside, missing
your amusing life somehow, and forging a new path to the future,
while yesterday's rain, unknowing, now falls softly in memories that are
soon quite lost, diffracting sunlight now far from the earth.

You have been everything to me and yet nothing,
and if your words are never spoken, and were I to
make the telling mark that I dreamed so long ago
it would not mean more than the present echo
                    of what we always knew.
The pieces of days lived in sunlight and sound are long departed.
Wine wet with rain that falls again and again in the shadow of your word
        is the vintage of our blood, the vibrant bond of
                loyal transfusion, the heart of the matter,
                    and yet it is not yet strong enough.

***

84

Poem present

Note the lines that I speak now
sound just as I read them,
echo the shapes that I wrote then,
so hear welcome words of when
these thoughts were wrought.

Inked paper, these lettered shapes now,
not the sounds from remembered time,
long faded the mind that thought them.
Close the book and try to listen,
the lovely ink is just the sound of the mind.

The notes of now float free from then.
I thought I knew when damaged words
were wrung from this splendid heart,
and now I can't remember then,
or when this poem was nought.

***

Why it gets written and how

It's just to relieve the itch of mind,
he said, that I write. But then
it feels better and there I am with
this most peculiar thing
I can neither grasp nor understand.

Old T.S. said of that, "you fool,
you're always the last to know
what those scrapings from your mind
Are about, and what's more,
it's much better that way."

Another said he had no choice
when it came to him and asked,
with trembling voice, to be written.
A kind man, he could not refuse,
but vaguely acquiesced.

It's just something I have to say
to posterity and my fellow humans,
said one who had moved sharply away
from disciplined discourse and finally
disembowelled himself on the page.

But still I ask myself, without success,
where these poems come from,
why I love them, what they are –
release, confession, unburdening,
lifted by the words themselves?

Assumed into another heaven
that may not be real, perhaps a real fake.
How can you know, as one who grasps
at shards of fractured dreams,
trying all too hard to learn how to see?

***

A Hostage of Time

If you think of all things as set in the order
of time, marked for museum's wooden drawers,
look for the telltale signs of subtle defect
in the fabric that entwines your arms and mind.

Look at the trees and the color of your lover's skin,
look at the intricate network etched on the palm
of the wintery world's enormous hand,
look for a change in the weather.

The snow will fly again, the west wind blow,
before the tumult of time's secret rancor can
touch you, take you hostage, carry you back
to the chaos of your world's beginning.

I stare at you wondering how long you can remain.
Your hands, softly veined, reach out to touch
my wrinkled cheek, then remember it's a good year
for apples like the one you gently hold.

The inadvertent vertices of life occur
in surprising, quick accidents of love.
though each complex day is no more,
you see me more or less the way I always was.

***

Children learn

It was the voice of amazement
that finally caught his mind.
Kindergarten is just too
serious not to be listening.
When did he first insist,
that it make some sense?

That insistent female tone,
thick with bright surprise,
draws him to discover
by solemn measure.
Children learn to desire,
their days filled with pleasure.

When did he first wonder
how she could be so surprised?
I want badly to be amazed,
long for the world in color.
That's now unexpected?
Can you help me to discover?

Tell me new things, like no others.
Tell me where the monsters play,
show me your secrets, perplex
me, alarm me, but make amends.
The hidden places are really few,
two tricky paths to timeless ends.

***

Cart song

The right reverend Martin was wont to say
that above all man's weaknesses stands delay
to arrest the downward slide of deliberate deed.

But in your gentle eyes it's clear to see
the awkward truth that lives in making,
the rhyme of thought and the color of feel,

the music of a rabid heart, play on aloud
and sing every song you know, sing them strong
before the cart of reality slides into the ditch.

***

A day of glory

The rising light of morning
glares into the solemn dawn
of glory's brightest day.

The wreaths of triumphant
deeds now gently rest
on honor's puzzled brow,

standing there dutifully,
adorned in droplets of sweat,
with an unflinching stare.

Wilting under the rule
of morning sun, honor
relents at last and comes to earth.

Rising to a brilliant star
the deadly heat brings sleep
to the afternoon.

I awaken at evening
alone in the meeting
darkness, to find that only

the pointless beauty of
these small accidents of time
remains, cooled in the night wind,
and finally it is just enough.

***

Summer's end

In frantic moments the widow wept with joy,
like the howling of that dog that drives you nuts,
like the ringing, brief sound thin glass makes
as it shatters. She could not believe
her good fortune, we couldn't believe our ears.

Yesterday it rained and people were depressed -
it means that summer's really gone.
We didn't believe when the leaves began to fall,
when the cool air circled and chilled our cheeks -
It takes more than that for the people around here.

But the cold cloak of darkening rain succeeds
where plant life and air get no credence - here
where green envelops all in summer like
today's cold coat, without remorse,
in greys and wet astride the bleeding earth.

But timing's poor as always,
and bound to find us still unready for hard,
new things. Around here life sticks in place,
longing for more of the same, wondering
if the metronome of days is all there is.

They pray there's more to their lives
than the passing of the season. People start
to turn to the hearth to nourish their ragged
dreams about now, to digest the warmth
of the summer crop into the fat of autumn
against the hard days that are to come.

We visit some mornings and exchange ripe thoughts
picked from our dying orchards. We have
subsumed, like the wondering widow, the pain
of harvest's grief, wakened by the cold rain's touch.
It should be just enough to comfort us
in the coming silence of winter's night

***

African tale

Endless ground, dust and time
so big you can't imagine
how far, how long you could go on.

Queen of time not renewed,
change, marked forever like a scarred face,
      hides at the forest's edge, all alone.

Her face turned towards me suddenly
in fear and surprise, growling cruelly,
baring teeth and hissing fetid breath,

I have come too close, I can see
the monstrous sin, the change
that ripped, reshaped her flesh.

I can see the lust of blood and terror
in her turned, narrow eyes.
Time renews only time, but change

doles out flesh and time in ample
measure now, as always, scars on scars,
mercifully the grizzled whiteness

vanishes, back into the dusty trees
until it can flick the hood aside and
reclaim in dying the rightful beauty of its mark.

***

The Flowers of Ending

It is your birth right to know
that the flowers of ending grow
in the mulch of discarded dreams.
They stretch to flourish full
from fetid earth to color pure.
Their smell is sickly sweet
with the stink of death,
I love them so.

In daylight they sublime to
the sun to burn and bloom
in the eye of voluptuous
splendor's momentary blaze,
and close, languid, resigned and
spent, when light has gone.
Their beauty is delicate
as the curve of the knife's blade.
Let us come to cut them in the morning.

***

Hospital stay

I am the eye of deadly morning.
Look back at me when I blink -
relent, and I am gone -
the streak of pale color
on the cheek of death's child.

A handful of sand,
hold it tighter
it's gone faster.
Substance of my soul,
it is confined
in the tightening turns
of forgotten pain,
or was it rapture?

It must be morning,
you're here with me.
The patient's pulse is strong,
and I am the delicate
ears of the afternoon -
listen for the sounds
of the breaking day -
the touted crack of
fractured, early light.

I can no longer bear
the thought of no
more visits -
I am the glow of
watery daylight
near the end of
a very hard week -
I am almost gone,
almost forgotten.

***

Afternoon's work

In the time of the morning paper,
echoes of your voice, and angry vowels,
words from the man I was meant to be, are muffled
by today's awful weather.

People of the other world can be heard
Laughing, softly behind that curtain.
I know a few of them – well lost
in the dark folds of the afternoon.

Clattering feet and the crowding press
of their other destinies, are also lost, but
in silence, in shouting and wondering
if this is the place or if there even is one.

Who will speak for them and for the other me?
I avert my gaze from the gusting wind,
pull my scarf up across my cheek
and hope they'll catch the eye of someone else.

***

Night comes to a Western Shore

The western shore soaks in the ends of days
and crumbles slowly beneath my feet.
light is dying hard, but memory
of morning lives in shards of sunlight between
shadows that stalk the settling sky.

On graveled bluffs of yellow stone
I watch with fear and wait
from restless vantage to stare
into the dim remaining glow
that lingers deep in my eyes.

A remnant touch, a soothing palm,
the last softness in the world,
slips reluctantly away.
The living hearts of yesterday's
deeds do not die in silence.

Darkness clots and falls in pieces
cloaking our vestige refuge

from the world as blackness fills my eyes,
slowly, slowly to stem the pain.

It's ending, now it's ending
though I cannot see,
I hear the hissing moan of light
leaking into the beyond that lives now
only in fragile dreams of my lost hours.

***

Japan

I.

The clouds build up
beyond the ridge,
bulging full
of white and grey.
The storm will slake the
land, but I long now for
the warm sun of morning.

II.

Your voice was like
the lace-white falls
across the lake when
you told me of your love.

III.

The leaves of spring
have faded into time.
The river holds no water
from other years, yet
we are still the same,
undiminished and
warming to the change.

IV.

The purity of moonlight
shames the face of those I love.
If it could touch their hearts
they would freeze like
the garden pond at midnight.

V.

My remembrance
gathers like drifting snow.
it pushes high against the fence
and covers blackened stones.
I am alone, but the birds
will return in the spring.

***

Novosibirsk

It is snowing with a casual air
that knows each flake will last
the winter. Forest stands in frozen
phalanx, glazed with the morning frost,
a noble, bristling white wall.
Each week the snow rises higher until
the remembered gold of autumn dies
a sleepy death in cold memory's reach.
Was it ever like this before? Were we
ever men of flowers, cities and warming light?

Visions of deep winter dreams intrude,
wolves and sledges, the desperate
sweep of endless Siberian woods,
arrogant birch and fir that stand around us,
relentless, they assail our every breath.
In bone-cold, crystalline air of the Asian
plains we now walk, cocooned and
herding all our fears before us, footfalls
unforgiving, muffled in the snow -
step by step, wondering in the darkness.

It is snowing at an even pace
without a breath of wind, no touch
of warmth, on the white silk bark,
a glimpse of intricate rime.
The silent forest rises, a huge cold idea.
Pale light seeps for a moment
into the battleship sky, strikes
the dust of a million tiny jewels
on the clearing ahead, and is gone.
We quicken our pace past the deathly
frost of our silent, brooding sleep,
                    and tread onward.

***

Mud Grass

Don't talk to me now, I'm cold and depressed.
The mud is indifferent black, but glazed
with films of wrinkled ice these mornings,
marked with lines from an unknown plan.

I am astonished at the memory of my former self,
bursting with blood, throwing open the window
rough and smiling hard into the fine day.
The weather has been frightful for weeks, and

life begins to molder away, sour and waiting
in chill shadows of the depths of March,
for someone's feeble signal recalling
forlorn dreams that breed in memory's dark distain.

Like the green whiskers of the water spirit,
dancing on the promise of deep, wet clay,
He seeped for days into the faintly warming earth,
and the grass came all at once at the end of the day.

***

In the morning

Today I've seen what I couldn't see before.
To rise quickly, walk on aching heels,
to tread cool floors and feel the summer light
at the window, brew coffee, strike
a blow at the chaos of my desk,
water plants and watch them swell,
feel the shower's water brush me with
careless love. I see it splash the walls,
sparkle on my legs, strip dried sweat
and skin cells from my arms and chest
and run into the drain's waiting mouth.

My chromosomes descend
by thousands into the sewer's
dark maw and collide
with a million others,
enough to populate the land
in random couplings
with every morning's wash.
The ritual, fruitless matings of the city's
people in the putrid darkness below
are acts of unseen desperation.
Think of DNA unwinding
to make a sticky net that holds
for a moment the complex mark
of an unborn poet's life.

Four of mine, two from Mrs. Dichter,
one from that big guy up the street,
two more from that pretty girl
I sometimes see, enough to make
a transient life, and then it's gone.
A new one forms down the pipe,
too quickly passed to see her face,
too quickly changed to hear his voice,
 I laugh and scrub again to send
my minions into the depths
to where people mingle,

and love this city for its possibilities.

To walk on the windy ridge above the lake
And feel the moss accept my steps,
I push myself on before last light
To see farther than I have before
I remember well the world of morning,
draped in the bright robes of the possible,
too complex to understand, too sweet
to hear the millions of morning's children,
and the songs they'll never sing.
In the draining light I close on home.
They say there'll be sun again tomorrow.

***

The Fawn

Your face in my mind, soft bones
of hard beauty stir my heart.
That golden moon at your throat,
crystal leaves at your ears,
you are the deer in that fading fresco
from a long fallen world,
wan amber hues remain
that once struck love's vivid eye.

Symbol of something long lost
like a city fallen to the siege
after bitter years of hatred,
of which it was said that no stone
was left standing on another, and salt
was scattered on the ground
that flowers would never grow again

to remind the besiegers of their shame
as long as history and the earth remembers.
Fawns parade upwind in the meadow,
across the river from the ruins.
You can watch them from the window,
and in the spring flowers grow there now.
Salt will never last in the earth.

Years of rain leach it from us
and make us soft again,
but neither do the flowers last.
Sun burns ever on the ground.
Fawns seek the shadow of the trees
where they linger, sleep and hide.
The fresco fades in full sun.

***

Picnic

Blades of grass cut sunlight
into angled slivers of bright.
The wind bends weeds that stood
all night waiting for the moment
when bees would come to call,
or when you spread the faded
blanket over and crushed them
to the soft, warming earth.

Were we here before, or did the
sun efface all recall of that day
from the earth, from our blinded minds.
The light's so bright this time of year,
the days are so liquid and long,
and the meadow is still green
with its slicing blades of grass.

***

Fiery crash into the sea

We saw the water aflame by night, on TV,
a fleet of torn airplane scraps by day.
Soggy paperbacks, a seat cushion,
dead still on the sea and Long Island beach.

I can't recall so much foolish angst over innocent death.
Stuttering cries from the mouths of excited cats,
tears and accusations and grim press meetings.
Not that I approve, but really – what good is there
in crying for these people we don't even know?

They were gone in so few violent minutes,
a maelstrom of burned, falling screams in our mind's eye.
Oh, so they're a symbol to you – for you and your kid?
Ciphers of grief for those you love – but really,

should that be enough for us? Can we afford to care
who these killers are, who died and where they all will go?
when the bottom is scoured for flesh and plastic,
the metal shards collected and laid on concrete pallets,
we'll know why they all died and how those moments were.

Soon enough we'll hear the bells toll on the sea,
Soon enough for you and me, and the sun will rise and sink.
You'll live and then forget and walk the beach next summer,
Talk of other things, wait for evening, sicken and die.

Standing on the sand now to watch grey water wash
broken shells and scraps of clothes from the dead,
I feel the planet sink in watery darkness, but looking
up I know that there will be bright stars above the world
for all my remaining years.

***

Song for my Country

A nice guy, with a lot charm, they said warmly.
That was meant to calm our brooding doubts.
A conservative of compassionate mind, they said.
but defects like divining death, are hard to ignore.
Dante says there is a special circle of the inferno reserved
for those who start the wars, where the agonies of the dead
will torment them for eternity.

The utter absence of wonder in this shabby, fictive world,
defiantly deaf to reason's careful call, is dark and hard.
I thought I would never after childhood hear brags
of ignorance – but George brags long and hard.
The walk, with hands faced backward, speaks of a hard youth,
of painful doubt faced down— but not so painful as ours.

One man, or two, can cast wreckage across the land,
and into lives they never knew, nor souls of unseen shapes.
We know the wreckage is real, so painfully here that
the notes of simple cheers and sound bites echo as laments
for those who can no longer sing from the hymnals of narrow contempt.

I ask you George Bush, I ask you Dick Cheney,
can you stare, not flinching, into eyes that see no more?
Wonder in silence just what they might have been?
Can you sleep, dreaming of death and the comfort and allure of pain
for those who hate you? Can you live in this dream of death?
Dream, we beg you, rather of what could have been.

The sleep of reason sounds to some like a peaceful night,
as demons stir and count the graves of those who died unknown
so that small men, who have not understood us, nor the promise
of our infant land, may not fear what they do not comprehend,
will not be found wanting in the eyes of those who still cannot see.

Awaken, smell the burning skin. Now demons are full afoot
now they hunt for the flesh of men who call the question.
Pretense is a warning scream. Come, let's grasp our memories.
Let's cheer for the lives and deaths of those whose lives
                                        we never knew –

mourn for the dead and for the promise of yesterday's hope,
rejoice for the ring of reason's fond awakening,
despair the desperate laugh of reason's death.

The chorus sounds against the double knives of blind belief.
Sing to blunt the blades and shelter those who care,
for what we think could have been, for what we in our delusions,
we in our comfort and forgetfulness have almost lost.

Laugh, not too loud, at the drunken buffoons,
mocking reason's challenge at the gates of fate.
Sing the tyrants' marching song, and dream,
dream of their ultimate demise.

Hate ignorance, for ever will it rise and strike at your heart
if unwatched, and sing the songs from long ago,
when giants walked our land in wisdom,
singing magnificent hymns of freedom's ring.

Sing, keep on singing freedom's painful music,
sing in harmony with your brothers, sing in the key of reason,
never let die what could have been, the hope of what we are.

It will not die.

***

Time and Their Words

Time was when we moved along the ways
of sibilant words, remarking on the gently
singing rhymes of sheltered dreams and words
of those who went before, each wondering
all the lonely hours of those who, having
ever dreamed in the deep chambers of the night,
remained to sing in shadow songs of minor key.

When and where was that delicious time, and who
are we to stand now above their bones
to ask of their memories that they turn
time inside out to speak of private things
they will never know? Can we know
what they saw, what they understood, and
what their fine imaginations wrought?
Their music is past – their singing fading fast.

Their joy and pain echo dimly now, but
in our walking on their paths we often find
their words, lonely fragments of the
sorrows of their passing hours. Could we know
the causes of their love, their living sounds?
In midnight hours faces sometimes come to sing
with us, raising voices that we think we know.

They seek a precious minute more with us,
A chance to hold that ringing note, trying to
close tight circles of time, around our artless
and profligate waiting, to recall the grace
of their own youthful dance, to forget
the anguish of their gently decaying bones,
and the lust for time of those who have no more.

***

Frienze

Coming in the haze of morning's sun
fear of the past haunts the city streets.
Can I brave the day and search the churches?
Dare I feel it and probe into the deep,
time-layered crust of love and hate,
the tender cruelty and beauty of men's hands?

On gold rose walls of pliant stone
the sun throws a veil of light,
each day a new bride for the insatiable old city.
Lust for ideas and beauty yields to power
and blood on the brushes and stone.
At evening she shudders softly to herself.

Thick honeyed living light oozes from crevices.
Dark water walks under bridges into night.
Wandering blood-streaked streets I smell despair
and drop some coins into the hat of a man
                                    with no hands.

Turning towards the light of the piazza, I look
hard into the darkness and see the glowing eyes
of tomorrow – they are just alive, today.

***

Robes of Stone

Like a long forgotten kiss your face smiles at me,
the fond fineness of your mouth speaks endearments.
I have lost so much that your restore,
                              won't you stay a little more
to reweave the colored threads of our life's clothing for an hour,
to wrap ourselves in skeins of time's fibrous bed.

The gardens of Tuscany draw warm dreams from me
on winter afternoons in the twilight rain from Alaska.
The pall that settles on the streets is something itself,
not just the loss of light, the pretense of chilling air,
pigment of dark hills and shadows speaking low
that seep through time, licks at the edges of open minds.

Before the night comes on I want you to call for me,
call me back to tell me of your dreams, your agonies.
renew the candor of the summer wine in the hillside grove
long ago – tell me you remember the mottled light on stone,
our statues, cedar musk and the summer scent of dusty walls,

The heat of the earth rising at the end of our day,
seeps into our bones and bears away our pain.
What did we wear in those days, do you recall?
can you reprise your pain, can you remember my dreams?
how can we tell when evening is really here?
Can you feel the motion of the flowing robes of stone?

***

Are you alright?

Dinner over he lit the fire
against the quickening rain,
looked towards her, busy with savage
attention to something very small.
Let it not be true that it's only
the fear of another failure
that binds them, waiting
fretfully for a telling sign.

Their youths are past now, the pace quickens.
They pause as for a mirror in time to wish
they could settle in for an evening's
repose, let the fire subside, turn down
the music, weave an allegory
of each other's fears, a rich fable
of improbable dimension,
like the imminence of love.

The burnt logs settle, light plays on
faces staring out different windows.
Are they seeking what is gone, in silence,
longing for what might yet be born?
Are you alright? he quietly asks
then turns back to the guttering flame.
Firelight falls silently to the carpet,
And spreads out, searching.

***

Muse

And then, just when I thought
I would never feel again the fire
that burned my hypothamic self to ashes,
or paint another picture, or kiss another child,
she walked across the room at evening,
sat by the window, brushed her hair back like so,
sang a ballad's verse under her breath,
and smiled like she used to, like the world
was right again, and looked out at the trees.
I laughed, walked over and asked about dinner
as I touched her neck and saw the shining clouds.

***

Farm Pond

Clusters of brown leaves
clot the grey steel
pond. On variegated
surface they drift
in morbid array.

From the muddy bank
hear the distant
calls of unknown
birds drift in from
disheveled woods.

The sky's slate
is flawless
but north wind slips
inside my coat, and
pulls long shadows

in the face of the pond.
In chill resign
I pocket my hands,
wondering how many
more warm summers

I will watch
end like this.
Staring at my
flawed reflection,
my toes begin
to feel the cold.

***

St. Petersburg

There was a year, he said, when the river,
ash grey now, ran red down-river from
the prison. People sublimed in the night,
hearts shriveled and died, longing for them.
He looked at me and drove across the bridge,
daring me to speak, dreaming of Vanya.

The cold, crimson eddies glint in streetlight,
mark the river's course through a city,
that loves its dead, hears their screams,
and patiently waits for dawning light,
and still the Neva flows slowly past
the living, pale shadows of men.

Fontanka and Nevsky, hauntings
of a frozen lake in time, he whispered,
muster in endless ranks, and now march
in darkness across Malaya Nevka.
We must, he said, be content to dream
and wait, wait for the whitening of the night.

***

DAVID GALAS was born in St. Petersburg, Florida in 1944. He received his AB degree in Physics from the University of California at Berkeley, and his masters degree and PhD from the University of California as well. His deep interest in biology emerged shortly after his PhD degree in physics and most of his career has been in biological research. For many years he worked in academic research, at the University of Geneva, Switzerland and the University of Southern California. At the initiation of the Human Genome Project, which he participated in starting, he spent time in Washington D.C. working as a scientific administrator. He soon returned to research in the private sector and then to academia where he works today. He has travelled widely and lived in Europe for a number of years. He has sporadically published non-scientific work, like poems, but considers his art and literature very important o him, but very different from his science. He lives in Seattle, Washington with his wife. His sons and their families live in Eugene, Oregon and Tucson, Arizona.

THE TRUTH

ABOUT

HEAVEN

Questions Answered

By
Christine Pocza Backus

TABLE OF CONTENTS

Emanuel Lutheran Church
Tawas City, Michigan

This book is dedicated to my Christian parents who brought me to baptism and nurtured me in the Word, and to the Lutheran Schools I attended from first grade through my first and only year of college.

God is good and has blessed me beyond measure in both good times and sad.

I am eternally grateful!

EVERY KNEE SHOULD BOW!

Your attitude should be the same as that of Christ Jesus: Who, being in very nature God, did not consider equality with God something to be grasped, but made himself nothing, taking the very nature of a servant, being made in human likeness.

And being found in appearance as a man, he humbled himself and became obedient to death - even death on a cross!

Therefore God exalted him to the highest place and gave him the name that is above every name, that at the name of Jesus every knee should bow, in heaven and on earth and under the earth, and every tongue confess that Jesus Christ is Lord, to the glory of God the Father (Philippians 2: 6-11).

HEAVEN
Introduction

Then I saw a new heaven and a new earth...I saw the Holy City, the New Jerusalem, coming down out of heaven from God... The wall [of the city] was made of jasper, and the city of pure gold, as pure as glass. The foundations of the city walls were decorated with every kind of precious stone... [Jasper, Sapphire, Chalcedony, Emerald, Sardonyx, Carnelian, Chrysolite, Beryl, Topaz, Chrysoprase, Jacinth and Amethyst]. The twelve gates were twelve pearls, each gate made of a single pearl. The great street of the city was of pure gold, like transparent glass (Revelation 21:1, 2, 18-21).

Then the angel showed me the river of the water of life, as clear as crystal, flowing from the throne of God and of the Lamb down the middle of the great street of the city. On each side of the river stood the tree of life, bearing twelve crops of fruit every month. And the leaves of the tree are for the healing of the nations. No longer will there be any curse. The throne of God and the Lamb will be in the city and his servants will serve him. They will see his face, and his name will be on their foreheads. There will be no more night. They will not need the light of a lamp or the light of the sun, for the Lord God will give them light. And they will reign forever and ever. (Revelation 22: 1-5)

People have many questions about Heaven. Is it a real place? How do we get there? What will it be like? Will everyone go there when they die? Will we be reunited there with family members? Will we still be a "family"? Will we eat? Will we work? Will there be animals, and if so, will our pets be there?

Some years ago, on December 20, 2005, to be exact, ABC aired a documentary news special about Heaven. I was (not surprisingly) disappointed after watching this special because it offered no hope for people. In fact, in many ways it led people away from heaven rather than toward it. In this documentary Barbara Walters interviewed people from all walks of life.

The four main questions posed were:

1. "Is there really a Heaven?"
2. "Where is Heaven?"
3. "How do we get there?"
4. "Will everyone go there?"

At that time an ABC news poll reported, "Nine out of ten Americans believe that there is a Heaven and that they will go there when they die." Those statistics are still very much the same today (2020).

After watching this special I was amazed and astounded at the things people believe about Heaven. I was disappointed that most people, even members of the clergy, seem to believe and teach that we must earn heaven by being good and doing good things for God and our fellow human beings.

It makes my heart sad to see people being misled. In response I have, with the help of God and Scripture, tried to answer more clearly and truthfully the questions people have about heaven. We will never be able to completely comprehend what to expect in heaven until the day we as faithful believers are called home. But we do know from Scripture that it will be amazing and perfect. In the meantime, let me help you put your mind at ease by passing on to you the truth about heaven from Scripture.

IS THERE REALLY A HEAVEN?

The verses which I quoted at the beginning of this book from Revelation tell us that there indeed is a heaven.

Jesus refers to heaven when He tells His disciples, *in my Father's house are many rooms; if it were not so I would have told you. I am going there to prepare a place for you. And if I go and prepare a place for you, I will come back and take you to be with me that you also may be where I am* (John 14: 2, 3).

God does not reveal to us everything about heaven, possibly because it is beyond our comprehension. Rather, He speaks to us figuratively and uses comparisons which we can relate to. He describes it as a place of "many rooms". In the old King James version of the Bible John 14:2 reads, *In my Father's house are many mansions...* In Revelation 21: 1 we are told that at the end of this age there will be a new heaven and a new earth, and a city of gold and precious gemstones. Because we understand that gold and precious gems are beautiful, God uses those examples to help us visualize it and understand that it is an unbelievably awesome place.

Try to picture in your mind a street paved in gold, or a city gate made of a single pearl. I can't imagine a pearl that size, but it certainly would be beautiful beyond belief. What about the *river of the water of life, crystal clear and flowing from the throne of God*? And the throne of God will be much more beautiful than any throne of kings or queens we have ever seen or imagined in this life.

There are places here on earth where we can find crystal clear water, so we know it is beautiful and inviting. Trees on either side of a river are quite common, but the *"tree of life" (same tree as in Genesis 2:9) is described as one tree, but on either side of the river. Wow! How can that be? Can you visualize a crystal-clear river flowing under the trunk of the tree with its massive branches flowing out and above? The huge Sequoias and Redwoods that grow in California could possibly be comparable.

The first verse of Genesis states, *in the beginning God created the heavens and the earth.* With these words He is referring to the sky and the heavenly bodies - the sun, moon, stars, and planets. But this is not "Heaven" the eternal home God has prepared for all believers. Heaven, the place, is more often referred to in Scripture as a Kingdom or House, prepared for believers.

Examples from Scripture:

*surely goodness and love will follow me all the days of my life, and I will dwell in the **house of the Lord** forever.* (Psalm 23: 6)

*Blessed are the poor in spirit, for theirs is the **kingdom of heaven**.* (Matthew 5:3)

*Blessed are those who are persecuted because of righteousness, for theirs is the **kingdom of heaven**.* (Matthew 5:10)

*The Lord will rescue me from every evil attack and will bring me safely to his **heavenly kingdom**.* (2 Timothy 4:18)

*"As the tree of life grows from both sides of the river, eternal life grows forever from grace. At Eden God placed Cherubim and a flaming sword flashing back and forth to guard the way to the tree of life (Gen. 3:34). But in heaven we will again have access to this tree." (The Peoples Bible, Revelation)

WHERE IS HEAVEN?

We tend to think of Heaven as being above us. The book of Acts describes the events after Jesus ascension - *he was taken **up** before their very eyes, and a cloud hid him from their sight. They were looking intently **up** into the sky as he was going, when two men dressed in white stood beside them. 'Men of Galilee,' they said, 'why do you stand here looking into the sky? This same Jesus, who has been taken from you into heaven, will come back in the same way you have seen him go into heaven'* (Acts 1: 9-11).

Jesus' description of judgment day also states, *they will see the Son of Man coming on the clouds of the sky...* (Matthew 24:30). We therefore picture Jesus coming back to us from above and think of heaven as being above the earth.

In answer to the second question, "where is heaven?" – we simply do not know because God doesn't tell us.

We could safely assume that it is another dimension which we cannot see with our human eyes. It is likely all around us.

God has given humans physical bodies and placed us in a three-dimensional world (height, depth, width). He does not give us the ability to see or comprehend anything beyond that. Although we can't know for certain where heaven is, it is comforting to think of our loved ones in heaven as being close by even though we are not able to see or touch them.

Our loved ones -
near, but yet so far...

HOW DO WE GET TO HEAVEN?

As I watched the ABC news special about heaven and listened to statements made by Catholic Priests, Christian Pastors, and Jewish Rabbis, I heard many opinions, but all were disappointing. Of all these men and women theologians who have supposedly studied Scripture extensively, only one spoke up with the truth and that was Evangelical Joel Olsteen. He stated (although hesitantly), "we are saved through faith in Jesus". He was correct.

The truth is amazingly simple. We are saved by God's grace through faith in His one and only Son Jesus Christ. It seems that in all their years of study and time spent in God's Word, these teachers missed the point completely.

Many discussed how one must be a good person - reaching out and helping others, be a good citizen, do not break the law, go to church, etc. But I ask you, *how good is* "good"? There is no human who is perfect. How does one know when "good" is good enough? God expects perfection. He tells us, *be holy because I, the Lord your God, am holy* (Leviticus 19:2). Sin is sin and it doesn't matter what the sin is, it condemns us in God's eyes. We are told in Romans 6:23, **the wages of sin is death.**

You may have never murdered anyone or robbed a bank, but because of that little lie you told, the gossip you shared about someone, that evil thought or hatred you felt in your heart toward another human, or the lust you felt toward someone you were not married to, you stand condemned in God's eyes. So, if that is the case, how does anyone get to heaven?

It comes down to that one little Bible verse we all know so well, but yet take for granted, *for God so loved the world that he gave his one and only Son, that whoever believes in him shall not perish but have eternal life. Whoever believes in him is not condemned, but whoever does not believe stands condemned already because he has not believed in the name of God's one and only Son* (John 3:16, 18). It does not get any clearer than that.

We inherit sin from our parents and their parents before them all the way back to Adam and Eve, the first people God created. Humans cannot obey God's law perfectly. But Jesus did it for us. He lived the perfect life that humans, because of their sinful nature, are unable to live. Out of love for us He chose to suffer and die in our place. He took the punishment we deserve for our sin upon Himself and gave us His holiness. In doing so He paid our debt to God. His blood, shed on the cross for us, washed us clean and made us fit to stand before a holy God. Plainly stated, we attain heaven through faith in Jesus who made us holy by His blood, shed on the cross for our sins. Re-read that verse from John 3:16, 18.

WILL ALL PEOPLE GO TO HEAVEN?

The answer is "no". Jesus tells us, *not everyone who says to me, Lord, Lord, will enter the kingdom of heaven* (Matthew 7:21). People may say, "I believe there is a God". But James 2:19 reminds us, *you believe that there is one God – Good! Even the demons believe that – and shudder.* Saying or admitting there is a God is not faith. *Now faith is being sure of what we hope for and certain of what we do not see* (Hebrews 11:1). Please read the whole chapter of Hebrews 11 to get a better picture of what it means to have faith in God.

Only those who sincerely believe in Jesus as their Savior from sin and come to Him with a repentant heart will receive His gift of salvation when their life here on earth is over. *And without faith it is impossible to please God, because anyone who comes to him must believe that he exists and that he rewards those who earnestly seek him* (Hebrews 11:6).

The second half of that verse from Romans 6:23 on page 17 reads, ***but the gift of God is eternal life in Christ Jesus our Lord.*** Salvation (heaven) is a gift of God's grace through faith in Jesus, His one and only Son. The apostle Paul tells us, *For it is by grace you have been saved, through faith – and this not from yourselves, it is the gift of God – not by works, so that no one can boast* (Ephesians 2:8, 9).

The word **grace** means **undeserved love.** God, by grace, loves us even though we do not deserve it. He loves all people, even those who do not profess loving Him. He wants all people to receive His gift, but those who reject Him will not receive it. *This is good and pleases God our Savior who wants all men to be saved and to come to a knowledge of the truth* (1 Timothy 2:3,4).

Heaven therefore, is a gift rewarded to all who by faith believe in Jesus, God's one and only Son, as their Savior from sin. Jesus is God in human flesh. He came to earth and lived the perfect and sinless life we are unable to live because of our sinful human nature, and He suffered and died in our place so that we can live forever with Him in heaven.

Sadly, not everyone will go to heaven when they die. God's gift of grace is for all people, but only those who die in faith will receive it.

The Holy Spirit puts faith in our hearts through baptism and through hearing, reading, and studying the Word. *Consequently, faith comes from hearing the message, and the message is heard through the word of Christ* (Romans 10:17).

Open your gift of grace and find life!

God's Word,
The Bible

If you don't know Jesus and are unfamiliar with God's Word, grab a Bible and begin reading. I recommend the NIV (New International Version) but others are good also. There is much in Scripture which may be difficult for you to understand, but what you need to know for your salvation is clearly written so that even a child can understand it.

The Bible is made up of 66 different books. The first books of the Old Testament beginning with Genesis tell us how God created the world and the first people, how the first people fell into sin, and the promise of a Savior. The New Testament tells us the life-giving Gospel message, which is the Good News of how Jesus, that promised Savior, came to rescue sinners from eternal death.

The Bible is God's story of the history of the world. When you separate the word "History", it reads, "His-Story". It is God's story from beginning to end.